I Spy Flint

ANDREA LOYD

Published by

Harper Book Publisher

www.harperbookpublisher.com

Printed in the United States of America

"To my mother and father

who never stopped believing in me and pushed me to my full potential."

Acknowledgment

First and always, thank you, Tiny Tunes Child Care, for making this vision come to life.

To my children, who are my heart living outside my body, you inspired me with boundless imagination.

I would like to thank Harper Publishing for their support and guidance.

To the readers, thank you for giving my character a home in your imagination.

To my close friend Lashawndra Johnson, thank you for providing encouragement, ideas, and feedback.

About the Author

Andrea Loyd is a wife and mother of three children. She enjoys spending time with her family and friends.

She was born and raised in Flint, MI, and graduated from the University of Michigan-Flint with a Bachelors Degree in Sociology. She also graduated from Baker College with an

Associates Degree, Early Childhood Education, where she found her passion for working with children.

She was a teacher for 10 years and started her own child care, "Tiny Tunes Child Care," to further her entrepreneurship dreams. Reading books in the classroom and child care inspired her to start the "Tiny Tunes Book Collection."

Andrea's education and background have provided many opportunities for her to give back to her community.

A tale of Tuni (Too-nee) and her exciting explorations

The sun rose over the magical city of Flint, and Tuni, a bright and confident little girl with two curly ponytails, was ready for her day of adventure.

FLINT
VEHICLE CITY

Tuni steps into the heart of Flint, where four magical colleges stand tall, each holding its own special mysteries.
What exciting things do you think will she discover in each of these magical places?

MICHIGAN STATE UNIVERSITY
M FLINT The University of Michigan-Flint
Kettering University Learning Commons
MOTT COMMUNITY COLLEGE

Tuni's heart swelled as she thought about all the travelers welcomed from far and wide at the Bishop International Airport of her beloved city, Flint. Where would you fly if you could hop on a plane?

Tuni rushed to the hospitals because she always believed that hospitals help heal hearts and that helping others was among the most important things in the world.

McLaren
McLaren
FLINT
EMERGENCY
HURLEY MEDICAL CENTER

Tuni's journey then brought her to the bustling halls of Genesee Valley Mall. What treasures will Tuni find here? What would you pick if you could choose anything?

FLINT
FARMER'S
MARKET

Tuni's little feet made their way along the Flint River Water Trail. She twirled and danced along the trail, imagining the river leading her to new discoveries. What creatures might live in the river's waters, and what secrets might they hold?

Her adventure then led her to The Flint Institute of Art, where the vibrant colors of the paintings dazzled her eyes, and the sculptures seemed to tell their own stories.
What kind of art will you create if you let your imagination run wild?

FLINT INSTITUTE OF ART

In the heart of Flint's market, Tuni smelled the delicious scents of fresh fruits and vegetables. Tuni carefully selected her favorite fruits, imagining all the different ways she could enjoy them.

Can you spot your favorite fruit or vegetable at the market?

EBT
STEADY
EDDY'S
VEGGIE
S MARKET
FLINT
Farmers'
Market

After all her adventures, she really needed a moment of peace and a place to relax away from the bustling city, and guess what? Tuni found a cozy corner in Flint's library, a quiet place full of stories just waiting to be discovered.

What magical tales do you think will she discover? What stories will you read next?

FLINT PUBLIC LIBRARY

As the day started to wind down, Tuni danced her way to the "Back to the Bricks" celebration. Classic cars lined the streets, their shiny paint glistening in the evening light.
What car would you choose to ride in if you were here?

FLINT
VEHICLE CITY

What could have been more pleasant than stopping by The Crim, a vibrant event that brings the community together to celebrate health and fitness?
If you lead a physical activity at the Crim, what would that be?

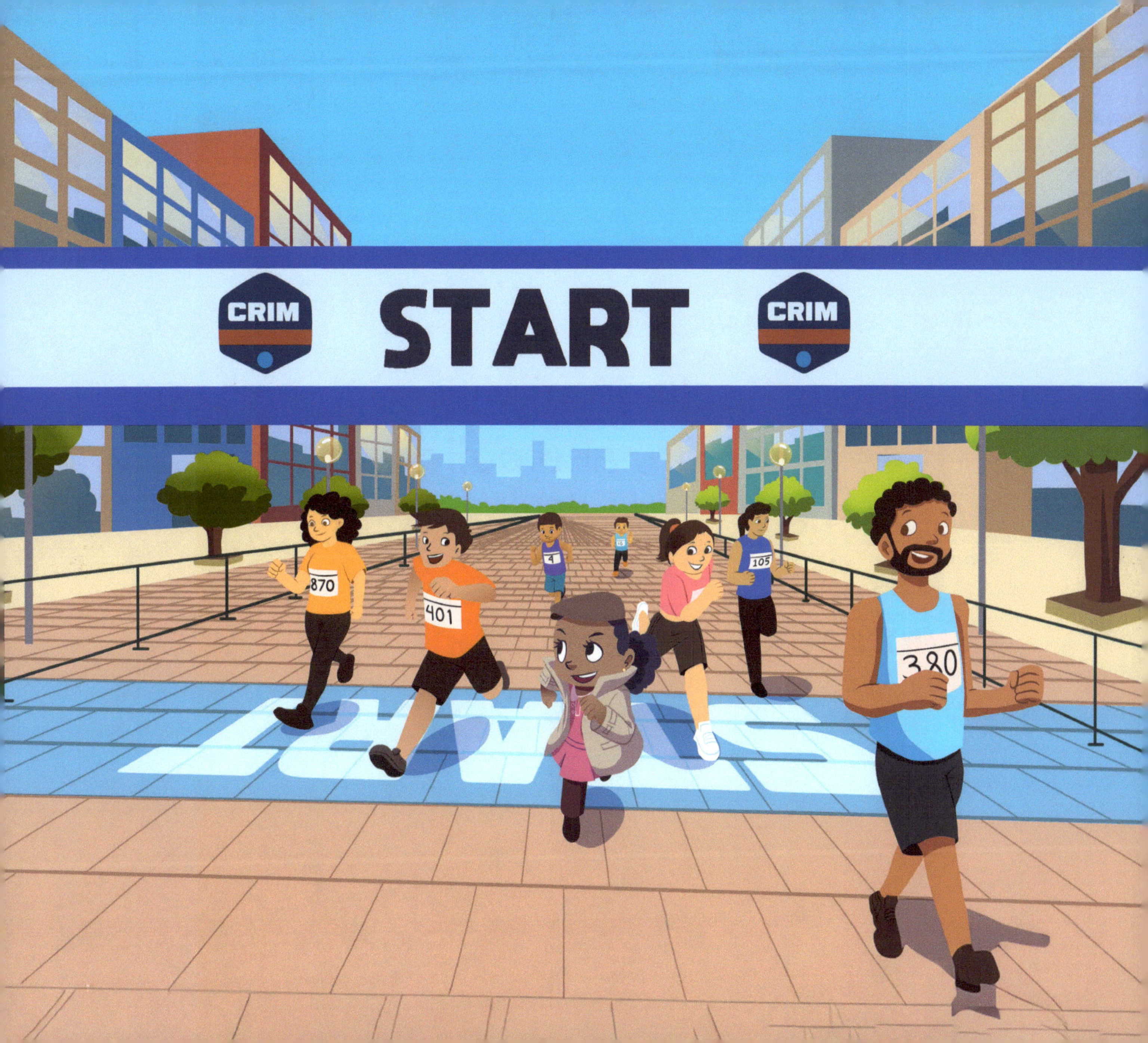

CRIM
START
CRIM
870
401
105
380

Hence, finally, Tuni visited the brave heroes at the fire and police stations. She gave them a nod of appreciation to the firefighters and police officers who worked to keep Flint safe and sound.

As the sun began to set, Tuni looked out over Flint, the city she loved. It had been a day full of wonder, learning, and imagination. She couldn't wait to see what adventures tomorrow would bring. What other secrets does the city of Flint hold? What will you spy next?

Tuni finds a special museum in Flint and starts an exciting adventure. She learns about how Flint grew from a small town to a big city and how cars were made there.
Each part of the museum teaches her something new, making her curious and excited to learn more!

SLOAN
MUSEUM
DISCOVERY

Thank you for joining Tuni on her "I Spy Flint Adventures." The adventure isn't over yet—there's still so much to explore! Keep using your imagination and see where it takes you!

FLINT
VEHICLE CITY

The End